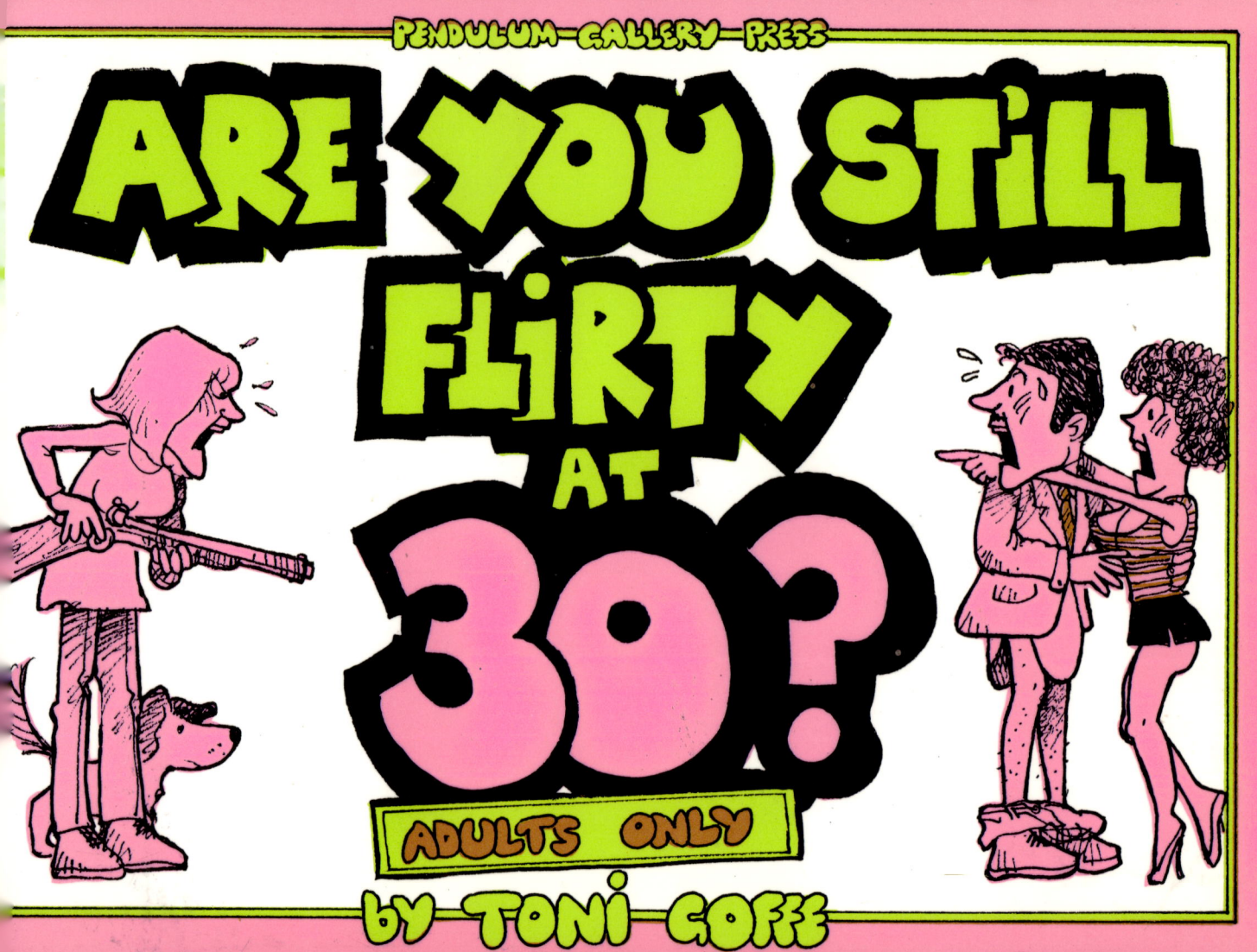

First published in Great Britain by
Pendulum Gallery Press
56 Ackender Road, Alton, Hants GU34 1JS

© TONI GOFFE 1988

ARE YOU STILL FLIRTY AT 30?
ISBN 0-948912-06-5

All rights reserved. No part of this publication may be reproduced or transmitted in any form or by any means, electronic or mechanical, including photocopying, recording, or any information storage and retrieval system, or for a source of ideas without permission in writing from the publisher.

REPRINTED 1988, 1990

PRINTED IN GREAT BRITAIN BY
UNWIN BROTHERS LTD, OLD WOKING, SURREY

"I DIDN'T KNOW YOU WERE SHY ABOUT UNDRESSING SANDRA?"

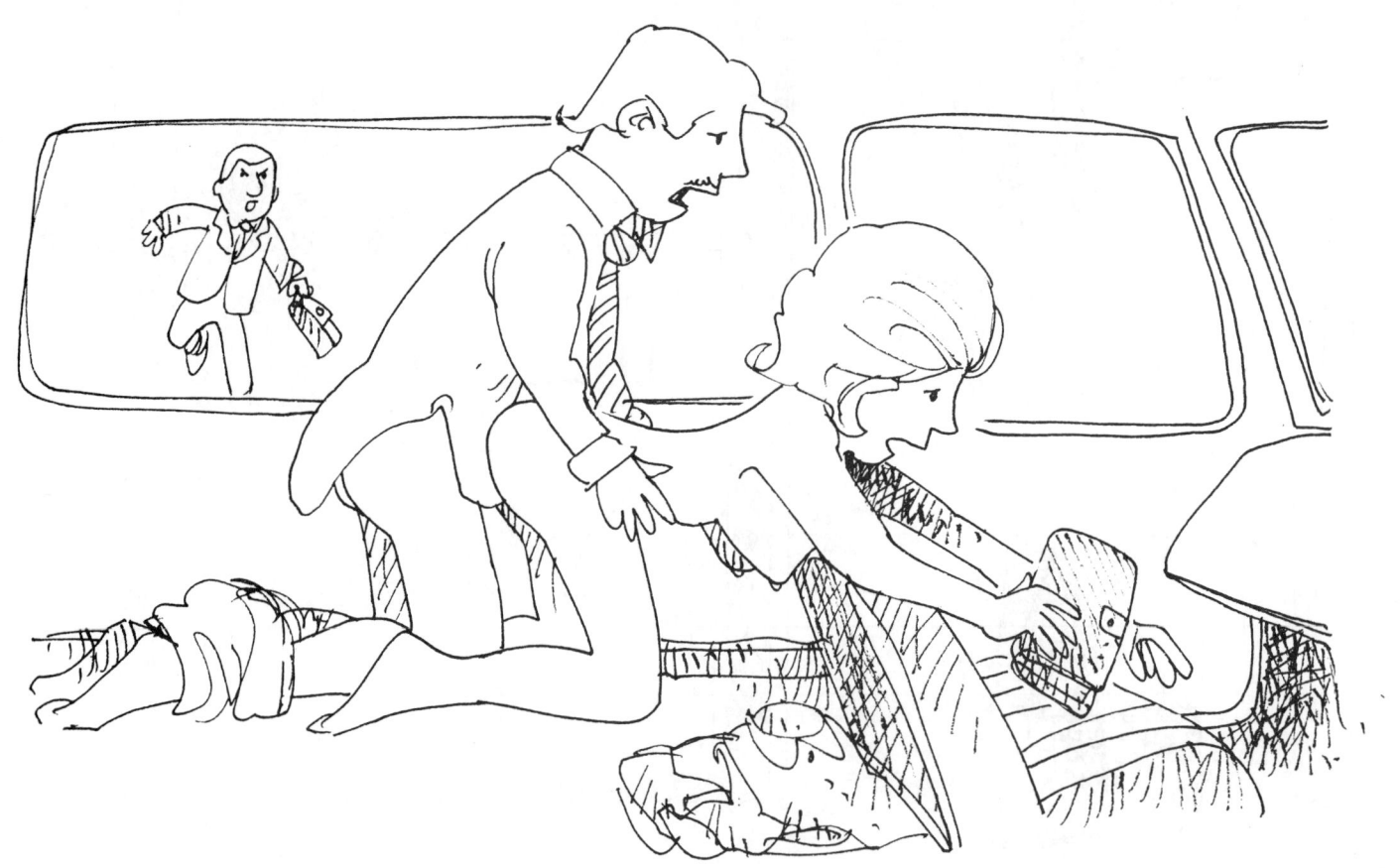

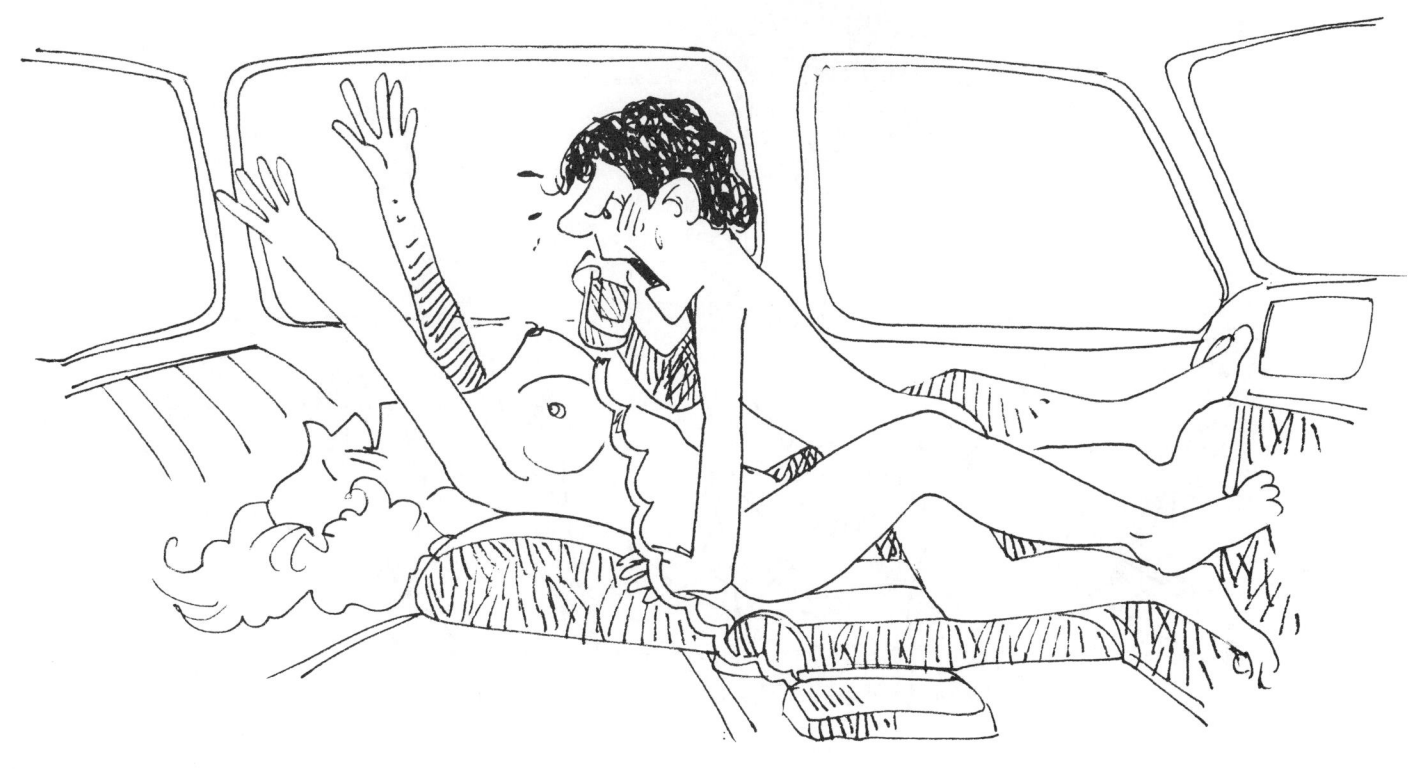

"I'M GIVING UP THIS JOB, I NEVER GET SEXUALLY HARASSED!"

"LISTEN DARLING, IT'S NOT WHAT YOU THINK....."

"HELLO RUPERT, HAVE A COCKTAIL, I AM!"

"YOU'RE RIGHT BRIAN, IT IS DARK ENOUGH TO CHANGE THE FILM IN MY CAMERA!"

—"GUESS WHAT? MY DOG HAS JUST HAD PUPPIES....."—

—"TAKE A LETTER—'DEAR SIR, REGARDING THE CHARGE OF SEXUAL HARASSMENT, MADE BY MY EX-SECRETARY....."—

"IT'S ALRIGHT SIR, I'M FROM THE NEIGHBOURHOOD WATCH COMMITTEE."...

-"WATCHOUT MISS SMYTH, THERE'S A HAZARD TO YOUR DRIVING COMING UP!"-

"WELL, WE CERTAINLY HAVE AN UPWARDLY MOBILE SITUATION HERE......."

"DONNA, ARE YOU SEEING SOMEONE ELSE?"

-"I DON'T REALLY LIKE THIS, BUT IT'S JUST SUCH FUN FOR MY FINGERS....."-

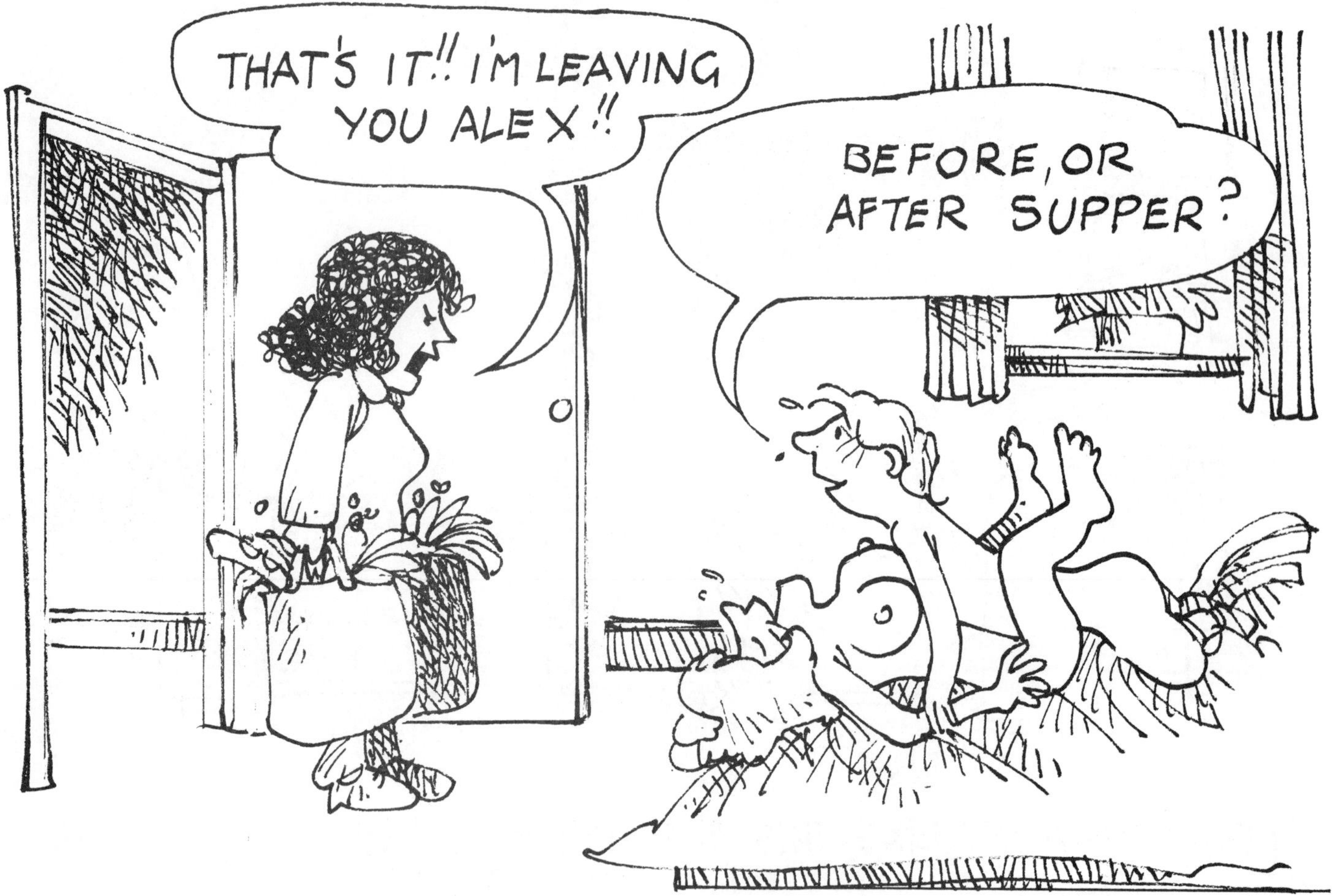
THAT'S IT!! I'M LEAVING YOU ALEX!!
BEFORE, OR AFTER SUPPER?

"ENJOY YOUR TAKE-AWAY — I'M BEING TAKEN AWAY TOO — GOODBYE!"

"ROGER, IS IT STILL SILLY OF ME TO HARBOUR SECRET HOPES OF RECONCILIATION…………"

THIS IS A TRAGIC SQUANDERING OF HUMAN POTENTIAL SHARON...
WHATEVER YOU SAY DEAR....

"YOU SEE, DOCTOR, MY MARRIAGE IS HAVING AN IRRETRIEVABLE BREAKDOWN...."

I'M LEAVING AND STAYING WITH MY BEST FRIEND WENDY...
THAT'S WHERE I'M GOING.....

IT'S DIVORCE CLIVE, I'M TAKING THE KIDS AND THE DOG!
THAT JUST LEAVES ME THE AU PAIR...

"YOU KNOW THOSE STORIES ABOUT THE HUSBANDS BEST FRIEND RUNS OFF WITH HIS WIFE - WELL, IT'S HAPPENING AGAIN!"

-"WELL, THAT'S HANDLED MY PROBLEM FOR THE MOMENT, Mr JONES NOW, ABOUT YOUR DIVORCE....."-

"MUMMY, DEREK'S DIVORCING ME, I'M COMING TO LIVE WITH YOU AND DAD!!"

"—"CUSTODY OF THE CHILDREN? NO! I WANT CUSTODY OF OUR AU PAIR"—

—"LOOK WHAT I FOUND. MARRIED TO MY BEST FRIEND!"

"BOY, WHEN YOU GET A MAN BRENDA, YOU REALLY GET ONE!"

"ARE YOU TWO GOING TO PLAY TENNIS OR WHAT......?"

"BOYS, I DON'T THINK YOU'VE GOT THE RIGHT IDEA ABOUT MIXED DOUBLES ...."

WITH THESE PRIVATE LESSONS, YOUR GAME SHOULD IMPROVE IN LEAPS AND BOUNDS..
DON'T YOU MEAN IN BUMPS AND GRINDS

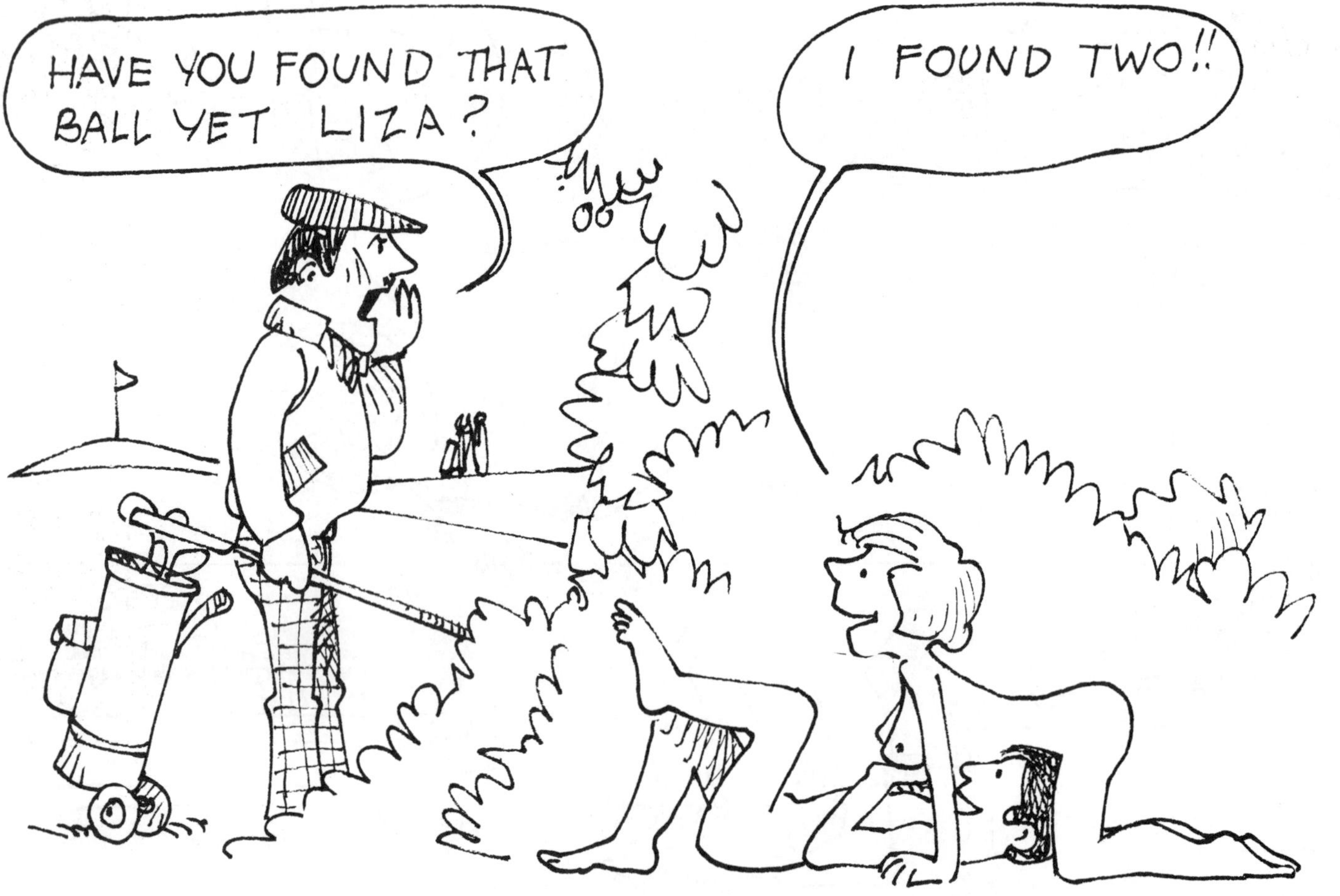
HAVE YOU FOUND THAT BALL YET LIZA?
I FOUND TWO!!

"HAVE YOU EVER THOUGHT OF GETTING A BIRD-BATH FOR YOUR GARDEN?"

"I LIKE GLASSES ON A MAN...."